Grieving, Sieving & Receiving

Puanani Holmes-Smith

BookLeaf
Publishing

India | USA | UK

Presentation by *BookLeaf Publishing*

Web: www.bookleafpub.com

E-mail: info@bookleafpub.com

ISBN: 9789357214629

First edition 2022

This book is dedicated to the future me who will need reminding that she has and will always have expression in her fingertips.

Internal Ablation

Sun speckled kisses
Soak through minds eye
Mini deaths
Exhaled icy breaths

Dragging feet
Panicky on the inside
Carpenter hands
Musicial instruments
Memories sifting sand

How can you be so skilled at beauty
yet abandon your creations
Grief in formation
Internal ablation

Blocked, bleak and heavy
Never once were you steady
Anger is not an emotion I feel
Except in your presence

Savage

Sweat drips off nose
Forehead scrunches tight
Muscles ripple as my mind cripples
sheer intensity slamming
weight against weight

I can't even look straight
Why did I think seeing you here
Wouldn't fire my desire
I hate what I admire
But only because I am tired

Tired of loving you and pretending it's easy
I ache till I'm almost queasy
My heart grabs hold
when alls done and told
I'm hoping edges fold
Why can't I be stuffed
into a package
Instead of reacting
So much like a savage

Beguiled

You're wild and you like it
I'm mild and I like it
My fire burns private
Only one way to sight it

Soft coaxing and gentle hands
Love spoken loud through wedding bands
Wild man trading hefty demands
Gruff throat whispering tender plans

Beguiled and I like it

Peace

Bad advice
Angry response
You love me but don't want me
Why would you stand in this place
With me
Hold me tight
'Look at me'
'LOOK AT ME'
how could you want that
when your words and actions
Ignore me

You hold me tight
What do you want from me
Beloved tormenter
Honestly
You say
But you do not want my love
Only the knowledge of it

Why would I give you
what you won't cherish
You say it's good
But you don't want it
Can't stand it

Don't see it
Won't be it

You call it fear
It's not beloved
You are blind
to the cost
Of loves steady hand
I have chosen to believe you
Release you
Unleash you
Make peace with you
All of you

Sore

I don't want to be here anymore
My heart is empty and utterly sore
You knock me down to my very core
When did life become such a chore?

Sideways

Sideways.

Backward, forward. Together, apart.

My heart sits sideways
to yours
and clings
to the ledge of your expression.

I wait for your acquiescence.
Motionless
except for the thumping drum
of your beat or mine.

It is all a blur.

Blurred lines and slurred words and honest
boundaries against half-heard lies.

You honest.
Me, a coward.

I love you comes out as
how are you
and

all I speak are lies.

Why do I lie when
all I want
is to be close.

Love. When did this become
a dirty word.

Me, honest.
You a coward.

I love
you.

I hate
you.

I wish I
hated you but
I am attached
to you
like a fishhook and if I leave it will ripe me
open.

You love me but not
how I ask.
You love me like you'd love anyone.
Quotedienne. Average

I am.

Just to you
a mirage.

Save me for I am
drowning
in this air that is not
made for me.
I cling and I cannot let go.
Hurt
me
so that I may know.

Suffocating is better
in water that
dulls
the noise.
I can float
here
without breathing.
Yes.

Let me
die
sideways
to the beat of my own blood.

For I do not have access to yours.

Mold Creep

Fear eats me and seats me
at the highway of hasty farewells
Sets tables for me
Sends cables for me
Blares train bells at me

Fear robs me as the sobs see
my breath
horizon hazy

Fear holds me
Like a cold weed
or mold creep
up walls of forgotten dreams

Fear trails me
With a stale greed
Grasping hold see
then a choked plea

Fear hates me
I resuscitate seed
Grown inside me
Trying to strain free

Though I hide need
Faith and hell bleed
with unquelled speed
I rise

You stamped labels on me
Killed fables in me
Made life all about me
But there's a new me

trying to out me
Laughter cloudy
soul confound me
I'm not yours anymore

Hefting sorrows bleak
dark encasements creak
I'm no longer meek
Listen up you freak

I will forage for my way
Letting courage send a tray
Carving storage out of graves
What a poor cage drawn in clay
Ever hoping come what may

You are too

When you ask me how I am
Are these just words or
do you give a damn

You say I'm amazing yet
 I'm pushed away
A journey so chaotic
threads are starting to fray

You call me scared but
you are too
What will it take for us to
speak the truth

My heart hangs so heavy and
 I feel so small
Waves pull me under as
I fight to crawl

Deaths days are over yet
I hear their call
Hurry up darling or
you'll start to fall

Found

When whispers of darkness sit in cloudy night
The knowing of another shifts the shadows light
Flicker by flicker, love blooms its tendrils
Hearts of stone grow weary, carrying hardness
tight.

"What can love do to me!" Shrills the early bird
Naive or naive, into fire spurred
Darkness and light, fire and stone
She knows not the weight of loves consuming
word.

Fire sloughing dross, rock birthing gem
Joy marks her moment, pain claims mayhem
Only reached through time and patience
Would one say yes to latent amen?

As if light spoke sound
Sunbeams sinking on dew-kissed ground
It asks all you have never mind price
How can one resist being utterly found?

Myself

I sleep by myself
Pregnancy pillow encasing
my yet to be filled body
Neck massager beating
My yet to be loved body

I eat by myself
Fat and protruding
hunkering swirls
Of distress and deep brooding
emotions left to rot and furl

I greet by myself
A rock alone in the waves
I am not strong, just tired
Too heavy to move to the lullaby
Now's the time for a hearty sigh

Salute

I have been filled with bitter fruit
My minds eye searing it's withering root
More than once have I given myself the boot
But nowhere else do I just quite suit

I tamper down the storm by calling it cute
This internal demon, this untamed brute
It can't only be me that it seems to loot?
Maybe the wind is blowing away all my fruit

I take a deep breath as life continues to confute
Even when its bleak and rainy there's a
substitute
So I hold on tight to this open-end parachute
Letting life swing me around as I give my best
salute

Alone

Today I am heading off to meet the father of
broken dreams.

You do not need to be there with me, beloved
husband. You do not even need to exist.

But I want you there.

Not as a crutch
Nor as a shield

Though you do uphold and protect.

Not as a warrior
Nor as a reprimander

Though you've healed by your strength and truth
in more ways than I can count.

Not as an excuse
Nor as a pawn

You are not my repeat attempt at wholistic
family.

I am a wild and strong woman. I will go no matter how hard. Restoration is in my hands. Generational curses break within my grasp.

I just don't want to do it alone.

Mead is that you?

Life's really thrown me
For a loop as it hones me
Into a pigeon hole of blown seed
Or perhaps a wooden crate turned sown mead

Bent back like rotten weed
drunk on need or greed or speed
Somehow hope's still able to plead

Jump on your trusty steed
gird yourself in study tweed
Let exhilaration take the lead
Find mead and creed and be freed

Christmas Treat

Dirty kitchen sick
Icy winter feet
Football match bringing heat

Spicy chicken meat
Edges of our seat
Roaring voices on repeat

Senegal is beat
Tomorrow another meet
Was this really our Christmas treat?

Sandy Riffs

In the windy waves
Working like mini slaves
Against the rocky cliffs
sit little crabs in sandy riffs

Poking holes for homey caves
Elaborate merge of dizzy maze
Back and forth in tiny tiffs
a lovely day of sun-kissed bliss

Leave me

It means something to me
A vow, a promise

Leave me for the one who sees me as more
beautiful than the sunset and more delicate than
the morning dew

Leave me for the one who loves me with an all
consuming passion and yet builds a hearth so we
can burn protected

Leave me for the one who loves my lips like a
promise and kisses like a vow

Leave me for the one who sees forever in the
curve of my chin and the stretch of my neck

Leave me for the one who yearns for me with
the patience of a monk and the ferocity of a king

Leave me for the one who would give
everything he is and everything he has to be near
me

Leave me for the one who would give me the
very keys to destroy him yet trusts that I would
never crush him

Leave me for the one who brings my soul to life
and fills my days with peace

Leave me for the one who challenges me and
does not withold loving truth

There is one who means something to me.
A vow, a promise.

Faces

Why do you want all these
faces?
You think you need them to
Survive
But really you just need to
Realize
That it's more important to have strong
Lines
To be intentional with each pair of
Eyes
No matter how big or small the
Size
To be surrounded by intimate
Cries
Of true relationship.

You must let go of all the
Traces
Of friendship filled with empty
Spaces
As if each new like helps you run the
Races
Each desperate click only makes you more
Faceless
Don't you know there is only one

Oasis?
I am your escape.

All to satisfy your need to be
Known
The desire for prestige constantly
Sown
Your heart's discontent substantially
Grown
All your ideas of happy unequivocally
Thrown
It won't satisfy.

I really wish that you could
See
I am the only one who can truly set you
Free
Why won't you relent and just be with
Me
You are not a burden.

Start looking at what we begin to
Create
This abundant life so deeply
Innate
This day I give you again a new
Fate
My grace is enough.

I am not the one who creates such
Division
Look at your history of my constant
Provision
Hear the cry of my gentle
Admonition
I want you.

My spirit walks with you as if like a
Dove
My tenderness knows no bound as I look from
Above
With unfathomable depths, I will claim you
Beloved
I died for you.

With great care I called you out of the
Waters
I walk with you daily as one of my
Daughters
The victory of Calvary can never be thus
Altered
So let's party.

Kingdom Man

Where you at, man of my heart?
I know the knot in the pit of your stomach.
I will help you burn, without burning up.

Where you at, righteous warrior?
Your battle is obedience and humility.
Do you see my ways? Listen to wisdoms voice
She will protect you as the sword strikes true.

Where you at, feet of the good news?
The weight of my calling doesn't stress you a bit.
Willing responsibility is different to obligation.
Like Hinds feet, leaping securely upon the
heights.

Where you at, lover of my law?
Integrity follows you daily, no persecution can
lead you astray.
Your kind answer turns away wrath, and
eldership sits at your feet.
The kings cannot make you bow even at the
table of death.

Where you at, covenant-maker?

I build millennia of faithfulness through your
seed.
A man of the mantle, covering his treasure all
his days.
The wife of your youth sits ever in your shade.

Where you at, kingdom man?

Rise

Come out of hiding
Designed for abiding
In the breathe, the wind
The sun's ardent skin

Rise up mighty warrior
I am with you
Leave masks behind
Hope is in you

Spicy Chill

Face aglow with rays
Rain pelts my back
Warmth and spicy chill
mixture filling me with thrill

Glorious Life

What will you do with this one
glorious life you've been given?
Will you squander it?

Will you ponder it?
Will you wander with hearts numb and
saunter through it?

Will you conquer it?
Standing tall on lifeless body.
Will you endure it? Obscure it? Secure it?

Or will you explore it with the rapture of forever
and the presence of this one, glorious moment?

* 9 7 8 9 3 5 7 2 1 4 6 2 9 *